The Fundamentals of Java-
Java at your fingertips

Kabir Mehboob

ISBN: 9798687157537

DEDICATION

Dear Abba, Finally after 1.5 year of hard work I made it, This book is dedicated to you as I am nothing without you, my existence my existence won't be conceivable without you, everything I learnt in my entire life was just your blessings nothing more than that, I Love you Abba and thank you very much for this life.

Introduction

Why choose JAVA ?

Java programs are portable across operating systems and hardware environments. Portability is to your advantage because:

• You need only one version of your software to serve a broad market.

• The Internet, in effect, becomes one giant, dynamic library.

• You are no longer limited by your particular computer platform. Three features make Java String programs portable:

1. The language. The Java language is completely specified; all data-type sizes and formats are defined as part of the language. By contrast, C/C++ leaves these "details" up to the compiler implementer, and many C/C++ programs therefore

2. The library. The Java class library is available on any machine with a Java runtime system, because a portable program is of no use if you cannot use the same class library on every platform. Window-manager function calls in a Mac application written in C/C++, for example, do not port well to a PC.3.The byte code. The Java runtime system does not compile your source code directly into machine language, an inflexible and non portable representation of your program. Instead, Java programs are translated into machine-independent byte code. The byte code is easily interpreted and therefore can be executed on any platform having a Java runtime system. (The latest versions of the Netscape Navigator browser, for example, can run applets on virtually any platform).Security The Java language is secure in that it is very difficult to write incorrect code or viruses that can corrupt/steal

your data, or harm hardware such as hard disks. There are two main lines of defense:

- Interpreter level:

- No pointer arithmetic

- Garbage collection

- Array bounds checking

- No illegal data conversions

- Browser level (applies to applets only):

- No local file I/O

- Sockets back to host only

- No calls to native methods Robustness The Java language is robust. It has several features designed to avoid crashes during program execution, including:

- No pointer arithmetic

- Garbage collection--no bad addresses

- Array and string bounds checking

- No jumping to bad method addresses

- Interfaces and exceptions Java Program Structure A file containing Java source code is considered a compilation unit. Such a compilation unit contains a set of classes and, optionally, a package definition to group related classes together. Classes contain data and method members that specify the state and behavior of the objects in your program .Java programs come in two flavors:

•Standalone applications that have no initial context such as a pre-existing main window

•Applets for WWW programming The major differences between applications and applets are:

•Applets are not allowed to use file I/O and sockets (other than to the host platform). Applications do not have these restrictions.

•An applet must be a subclass of the Java Applet class. Applications do not need to sub class any particular class.

•Unlike applets, applications can have menus.

•Unlike applications, applets need to respond to predefined lifecycle messages from the WWW browser in which they're running .Java Program Execution The Java byte-code compiler translates a Java source file into machine-independent byte code. The byte code for each publicly visible class is placed in a separate file, so that the Java runtime system can easily find it. If your programming initiates an object of class A, for example, the class loader searches the directories listed in your CLASSPATH environment variable for a file called a class that contains the class definition and byte code for class A.

The Fundamentals of Java

Contents........

- Runtime vs. Checked Exceptions
- Array List
- LinkedLists
- HashMap
- Sets
- Sorting Lists
- Iterators
- Working with Files
- Reading a File
- Creating and Writing Files
- Quiz- 006

Chapter 1 – Basic Concepts

1.0.0 Introduction to Java-

Welcome to Java!

Java is an elevated level, present day programming language planned in the mid 1990s by Sun Microsystems, and as of now claimed by Oracle.

Java is Platform Independent, which implies that you just need to compose the program once to have the option to run it on various stages!

Java is compact, powerful, and dynamic, with the capacity to fit the necessities of basically any kind of utilization.

Java

In excess of 3 billion gadgets run Java.

Java is utilized to create applications for Google's Android OS, different Desktop Applications, for example, media players, antivirus programs, Web Applications, Enterprise Applications (for example banking), and some more!

1.0.1 First Program- "Hello World !"-

How about we start by making a basic program that prints "Hi World" to the screen

```java
class MyClass {
  public static void main(String[ ] args) {
    System.out.println("Hello World");
  }
}
```

In Java, each line of code that can really run should be inside a class. In our model, we named the class MyClass. You will study classes in the up and coming modules. In Java, every application has a passage point, or a beginning stage, which is a strategy called primary. Alongside primary, the watchwords public and static will likewise be clarified later.

1.0.1.0 The main Method

To run our program, the fundamental strategy must be indistinguishable from this mark:

public static void main(String[ ] args)

- public: anyone can access it

- static: method can be run without creating an instance of the class containing the main method

- void: method doesn't return any value

- main: the name of the method

For instance, the accompanying code proclaims a strategy called test, which doesn't restore anything and has no boundaries:

```
void test()
```

1.0.1.2 System.out.println()

Next is the body of the principle strategy, encased in curly braces:

```
{
  System.out.println("Hello World!");
}
```

The println method prints a line of text to the screen.

The System class and its out stream are utilized to get to the println method.

1.0.1.3 Semicolons in Java

You can pass a different text as the parameter to the println method to print it.

```
class MyClass {
  public static void main(String[] args) {
    System.out.println("I am learning Java");
  }
}
```

In Java, each code statement must end with a **semicolon**.

Note: do not use **semicolons** after method and class declarations that follow with the body defined using the curly braces.

1.0.2 Java Comments-

1.0.2.1 **Comments**

The purpose behind including comments for your code is to clarify what the code is doing. Java underpins both single and multi-line Comments . All characters that show up inside a Comments are ignored by the Java compiler.

1.0.2.2 **Single-Line Comments**

A *single-line comment* starts with two forward slashes (//) and continues until it reaches the end of the line.

For example :

// This is a single line comment

Note: Including comments as you write code is a decent practice, since they give explanation and understanding when you have to allude back to it, just as for other people, who may need to understand it.

1.0.2.3 **Multi-Line Comments**

Java additionally underpins comments that range different lines. You start this sort of comments with a forward slash followed by an asterisk, and end it with an asterisk followed by a forward slash.

For example:

/* This is a

   Multi-line comment

*/

You also may import a single line comment into a nested multi-line comment

/* This is a

   //A single line comment inside multi-line comment

Multi-line comment

*/

Note: A multi-line Comment is also known as Blocked comment

1.0.2.4 Documentation Comment

Documentation comments are uncommon comments that resemble multi-line comments, with the distinction being that they produce outside documentation of your source code. These start with a forward slash followed by two asterisk and end with a reference mark followed by a forward cut.

For example:

/** This is a documentation comment */

/**

This is a documentation comment

*/

Javadoc is a tool which comes with JDK and it is used for generating Java code documentation in HTML format from Java source code which has required documentation in a predefined format.
When a documentation comment begins with more than two asterisks, Javadoc assumes that you want to create a "box"

around the comment in the source code. It simply ignores the extra asterisks.

For example:

```
/*********************

This is the start of a method

*********************/
```

Note: This will retain just the text "This is the start of a method" for the documentation.

1.0.3 Variables-

Variables store data for processing.

A variable is given a name (or identifier, for example, area, age, height, and so forth. The name interestingly distinguishes every factor, doling out an incentive to the variable and recovering the worth put away.

Factors have types. A few models:

- int: for whole numbers (entire numbers, for example, 123 and -456

- double: for drifting point or genuine numbers with discretionary decimal focuses and partial parts in fixed or logical documentations, for example, 3.1416, - 55.66.

- String: for writings, for example, "Hi" or "Hello!". Text strings are encased inside twofold statements.

You can declare a variable of a type and assign it a value.

For Example:

String name = "David";

This creates a variable called **name** of type **String**, and assigns it the value "David".

Note: A variable is related with a sort, and is just fit for putting away estimations of that specific kind. For instance, an int variable can store number qualities, for example, 123; yet it can't store genuine numbers, for example, 12.34, or messages, for example, "Hi".

Examples of variable declarations:

```java
class MyClass {
  public static void main(String[ ] args) {
    String name ="David";
    int age = 42;
    double score =15.9;
    char group = 'Z';
  }
}
```

char stands for character and holds a single character.

Another type is the **Boolean** type, which has only two possible values: **true** and **false**.
This data type is used for simple flags that track true/false conditions.
For example:

Boolean online = true;

Note : You can use a comma-separated list to declare more than one variable of the specified type. Example: int a = 42, b = 11;

1.0.4 Primitive Operators-
1.0.4.1   The Math Operators-

Java provides a rich set of operators to use in manipulating variables. A value used on either side of an operator is called an **operand**.
For example, in the expression below, the numbers 6 and 3 are operands of the plus operator:

int x = 6 + 3;

Java arithmetic operators:
+ **addition**
- **subtraction**
* **multiplication**
/ **division**
% **modulo**

Note: Arithmetic operators are used in mathematical expressions in the same way that they are used in algebraic equations.

1.0.4.2   Addition

The + operator adds together two values, such as two constants, a constant and a variable, or a variable and a variable. Here are a few examples of addition:

```
int sum1 = 50 + 10;
int sum2 = sum1 + 66;
int sum3 = sum2 + sum2;
```

1.0.4.3   Subtraction

The - operator subtracts one value from another.

```
int sum1 = 1000 - 10;
int sum2 = sum1 - 5;
int sum3 = sum1 - sum2;
```

Note : Just like in algebra, you can use both of the operations in a single line. For example: int val = 10 + 5 - 2;

1.0.4.4   Multiplication

The * operator multiplies two values.

```
int sum1 = 1000 * 2;
int sum2 = sum1 * 10;
int sum3 = sum1 * sum2;
```

1.0.4.5   Division

The / operator divides one value by another.

```
int sum1 = 1000 / 5;
int sum2 = sum1 / 2;
int sum3 = sum1 / sum2;
```

Note : In the example above, the result of the division equation will be a whole number, as **int** is used as the data type. You can use **double** to retrieve a value with a decimal point.

1.0.4.6   Modulo

The **modulo** (or remainder) math operation performs an integer division of one value by another, and returns the remainder of that division.

The operator for the modulo operation is the percentage (%) character.

Example:

```
int value = 23;
int res = value % 6; // res is 5
```

Note: Dividing 23 by 6 returns a quotient of 3, with a remainder of 5. Thus, the value of 5 is assigned to the **res** variable.

1.0.5 Increment & Decrement-

An increment or decrement operator provides a more helpful and reduced approach to increase or decrease the value of a variable by one.

For example, the statement **x=x+1;** can be simplified to **++x;**
Example:

```
int test = 5;
++test; // test is now 6
```

The **decrement** operator (--) is used to decrease the value of a variable by one.

```
int test = 5;
--test; // test is now 4
```

Note : Use this operator with caution to avoid calculation mistakes.

1.0.5.1   Prefix & Postfix

Two structures, prefix and postfix, might be utilized with both the increment and decrement operators.

With prefix structure, the operator shows up before the operand, while in postfix structure, the operator shows up after the operand. The following is a clarification of how the two structures work:

Prefix: Increments the variable's worth and utilizations the new incentive in the articulation.

Example:

```
int x = 34;
int y = ++x; // y is 35
```

The value of x is first incremented to 35, and is then assigned to y, so the values of both x and y are now 35.
Postfix: The variable's value is first used in the expression and is then increased.
Example:

```
int x = 34;
int y = x++; // y is 34
```

x is first assigned to y, and is then incremented by one. Therefore, x becomes 35, while y is assigned the value of 34.

Note : The decrement operator as well applies the same

1.0.5.2 **The Assignment Operator**

You are already familiar with the **assignment** operator (=), which assigns a value to a variable.

```
int value = 5;
```

This assigned the value 5 to a variable called **value** of type **int**. Java provides a number of assignment operators to make it easier to write code.

Addition and assignment (+=):

```
int num1 = 4;
int num2 = 8;
num2 += num1; // num2 = num2 + num1;

// num2 is 12 and num1 is 4
```

Subtraction and assignment (-=):

```
int num1 = 4;
int num2 = 8;
num2 -= num1; // num2 = num2 - num1;

// num2 is 4 and num1 is 4
```

Note : Similarly, Java supports multiplication and assignment (*=), division and assignment (/=), and remainder and assignment (%=).

1.0.6 Strings-

A String is an item that speaks to a grouping of characters. For instance, "Hello" is a string of 5 characters.

String s = "SoloLearn";

Note : You are allowed to define an empty string. For example, String str = "";

1.0.6.1 String Concatenation

The + (plus) operator between strings adds them together to make a new string. This process is called concatenation.

The resulted string is the first string put together with the second string.

For example:

```java
String firstName, lastName;
firstName = "David";
lastName = "Williams";

System.out.println("My name is " + firstName +" "+lastName);

// Prints: My name is David Williams
```

Note: The **char** data type represents a single character.

1.0.7 Quiz-001,

Q.1. Please type in a code to declare two variables of type int and print their sum using the sum variable.

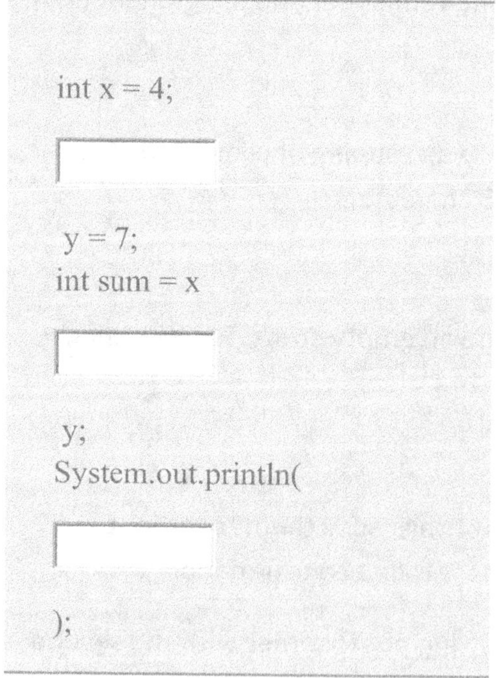

Q.2. In every Java program...

- all of the variables must be integers.
- there must be a method called "main".
- there must be at least two variables declared.

Q.3. Fill in the options below to output the name:

______name;

name = "David";

_______.out.println(______);

Name	int	System	Java	String

Chapter 2 – Conditionals & Loops

2.0.1 Conditional Statements-

Contingent statements are utilized to perform various activities dependent on various conditions.

The if statements is one of the most habitually utilized restrictive explanations.

On the off chance that the if statements condition articulation assesses to true, the square of code inside the if statements is executed. On the off chance that the articulation is discovered to be false, the main arrangement of code after the finish of the if statements (after the end wavy support) is executed.

Syntax:

```
if (condition) {

  //Executes when the condition is true

}
```

Any of the following comparison operators may be used to form the condition:

< less than

> greater than

!= not equal to

== equal to

<= less than or equal to

>= greater than or equal to

For example:

```
int x = 7;
```

```
if(x < 42) {

 System.out.println("Hi");}
```

Note : Remember that you need to use two equal signs (==) to test for equality, since a single equal sign is the assignment operator.

2.0.1.1 if...else Statements

An **if** statement can be followed by an optional **else** statement, which executes when the condition evaluates to false.

```
int age = 30;

if (age < 16) {
   System.out.println("Too Young");
} else {
   System.out.println("Welcome!");
}
//Outputs "Welcome!"
```

Note : As age equals 30, the condition in the **if** statement evaluates to false and the **else** statement is executed.

2.0.2 Nested If Statements

You can use one **if-else** statement inside another **if** or **else** statement.

For example:

```java
int age = 25;
if(age > 0) {
  if(age > 16) {
    System.out.println("Welcome!");
  } else {
    System.out.println("Too Young");
  }
} else {
  System.out.println("Error");
}
//Outputs "Welcome!"
```

Note : You can nest as many **if-else** statements as you want.

2.0.1.2 **Else If statements**

Instead of using nested **if-else** statements, you can use the **else if** statement to check multiple conditions.

For example:

```java
int age = 25;

if(age <= 0) {
  System.out.println("Error");
} else if(age <= 16) {
  System.out.println("Too Young");
} else if(age < 100) {
  System.out.println("Welcome!");
} else {
  System.out.println("Really?");
}
//Outputs "Welcome!"
```

The code will check the condition to evaluate to true and execute the statements inside that block.

Note : You can include as many **else if** statements as you need.

2.0.1.3 **Logical Operators-**

Logical operators are used to combine multiple conditions.

Let's say you wanted your program to output "Welcome!" only when the variable age is greater than 18 and the variable money is greater than 500.

One way to accomplish this is to use nested if statements:

```java
if (age > 18) {
  if (money > 500) {
    System.out.println("Welcome!");
  }
}
```

However, using the **AND** logical operator (**&&**) is a better way:

```java
if (age > 18 && money > 500) {
  System.out.println("Welcome!");
}
```

Note : If both operands of the AND operator are true, then the condition becomes true.

2.0.1.3 The OR Operator

The **OR** operator (||) checks if any one of the conditions is true. The condition becomes true, if any one of the operands evaluates to true.

For example:

```java
int age = 25;
int money = 100;

if (age > 18 || money > 500) {
  System.out.println("Welcome!");
}
//Outputs "Welcome!"
```

The code above will print "Welcome!" if age is greater than 18 **or** if money is greater than 500.

The **NOT (!)** logical operator is used to reverse the logical state of its operand. If a condition is true, the **NOT** logical operator will make it false.

```java
int age = 25;
if(!(age > 18)) {
   System.out.println("Too Young");
} else {
   System.out.println("Welcome");
}
//Outputs "Welcome"
```

Note : as "if age is NOT greater than 18".

2.0.1.4 The Switch Statement

A **switch** statement tests a variable for equality against a list of values. Each value is called a **case**, and the variable being switched on is checked for each case.

```java
switch (expression) {
   case value1 :
      //Statements
      break; //optional
   case value2 :
      //Statements
      break; //optional
      //You can have any number of case statements.
   default : //Optional
      //Statements
}
```

- When the variable being switched on is equal to a **case**, the statements following that **case** will execute until a **break** statement is reached.
- When a **break** statement is reached, the **switch** terminates, and the flow of control jumps to the next line after the **switch**

statement.

- Not every **case** needs to contain a **break**. If no **break** appears, the flow of control will fall through to subsequent cases until a **break** is reached.

The example below tests **day** against a set of values and prints a corresponding message.

```java
int day = 3;

switch(day) {
  case 1:
    System.out.println("Monday");
    break;
  case 2:
    System.out.println("Tuesday");
    break;
  case 3:
    System.out.println("Wednesday");
    break;
}
// Outputs "Wednesday"
```

Note : You can have any number of **case** statements within a **switch**. Each **case** is followed by the comparison value and a colon.

2.0.1.5 The Default Statements

A switch statement can have an optional **default** case.
The **default** case can be used for performing a task when none of the cases is matched.

For Example:

```java
int day = 3;

switch(day) {
  case 6:
    System.out.println("Saturday");
    break;
  case 7:
    System.out.println("Sunday");
    break;
  default:
    System.out.println("Weekday");
}
// Outputs "Weekday"
```

No **break** is needed in the default case, as it is always the last statement in the switch.

2.0.1.6 **While Loops**

A **loop** statement allows to repeatedly execute a statement or group of statements.

A **while** loop statement repeatedly executes a target statement as long as a given condition is true.

For Example:

```java
int x = 3;

while(x > 0) {
  System.out.println(x);
  x--;
}
/*
Outputs
  3
  2
  1
*/
```

When the expression is tested and the result is false, the loop body is skipped and the first statement after the while loop is executed.

Example:

```
int x = 6;

while( x < 10 )
{
  System.out.println(x);
  x++;
}
System.out.println("Loop ended");

/*
6
7
8
9
Loop ended
*/
```

Note : Notice that the last print method is out of the while scope.

2.0.1.7 **For Loops**

Another loop structure is the **for** loop. A for loop allows you to efficiently write a loop that needs to execute a specific number of times.

Syntax:

```
for (initialization; condition; increment/decrement) {
statement(s)
}
```

Initialization: Expression executes only once during the beginning of loop

Condition: Is evaluated each time the loop iterates. The loop executes the statement repeatedly, until this condition returns false.

Increment/Decrement: Executes after each iteration of the loop.

The following example prints the numbers 1 through 5.

```
for(int x = 1; x <=5; x++) {
  System.out.println(x);
}

/* Outputs
1
2
3
4
5
*/
```

This initializes x to the value 1, and repeatedly prints the value of x, until the condition x<=5 becomes false. On each iteration, the statement x++ is executed, incrementing x by one.

Note : Notice the semicolon (;) after initialization and condition in the syntax.

You can have any type of condition and any type of increment statements in the for loop.

The example below prints only the even values between 0 and 10:

```
for(int x=0; x<=10; x=x+2) {
  System.out.println(x);
}
/*
0
2
4
6
8
10
*/
```

Note : A **for** loop is best when the starting and ending numbers are known.

2.0.1.8 Do while Loops

A **do...while** loop is similar to a **while** loop, except that a
do...while loop is guaranteed to execute at least one time.
Example:

```
int x = 1;
do {
  System.out.println(x);
  x++;
} while(x < 5);

/*
1
2
3
4
*/
```

Notice that the condition appears at the end of the loop, so the
statements in the loop execute once before it is tested.
Even with a false condition, the code will run once.
Example:

```
int x = 1;
do {
  System.out.println(x);
  x++;
} while(x < 0);

//Outputs 1
```

Note : In do...while loops, the while is just the condition and
doesn't have a body itself.

2.0.1.9 Loop Control Statements

The **break** and **continue** statements change the loop's execution flow.

The **break** statement terminates the loop and transfers execution to the statement immediately following the loop.

Example:

```java
int x = 1;

while(x > 0) {
 System.out.println(x);
  if(x == 4) {
    break;
  }
  x++;
}

/* Outputs
1
2
3
4
*/
```

The **continue** statement causes the loop to skip the remainder of its body and then immediately retest its condition prior to reiterating. In other words, it makes the loop skip to its next iteration.

Example:

```java
for(int x=10; x<=40; x=x+10) {
  if(x == 30) {
    continue;
  }
  System.out.println(x);
}
/* Outputs
 10
 20
 40
*/
```

Note : As you can see, the above code skips the value of 30, as directed by the **continue** statement.

2.0.2 **Quiz-002,**

Q.1. Fill in the blanks to print "in a loop" 7 times, using the while loop.

```java
int x = 1;
while (x <=


) {
  System.out.println("in a loop");


      ++;
}
```

Q.2. Please select the correct statements about && and || operators.

- o a && b is false if both a and b are true
- o a && b is true if either a or b is true
- o a || b is true if either a or b is true
- o (a || b) && c is true if c is true and either a or b is true

Q.3. Fill in the blanks to print "You rock!" if variable "a" is greater than 15, and variable "b" is less than or equal to 72.

```
int a = 144;
int b = 33;
if (a > 15

[            ]

b <=

[            ]

) {
    System.out.println("You rock!");
}
```

Q.4. Fill in the blanks to print "in a loop" 5 times using the for loop.

```
[            ]

(int x = 0;

[            ]

< 5; x++) {
    System.out.println("in a loop");
}
```

Chapter 3 – Arrays

3.0.1 Arrays

An **array** is a collection of variables of the same type.
When you need to store a list of values, such as numbers, you can store them in an array, instead of declaring separate variables for each number.

To declare an array, you need to define the type of the elements with **square brackets**.
For example, to declare an array of integers:

```
 int[ ] arr;
```
The name of the array is **arr**. The type of elements it will hold is **int**.

Now, you need to define the array's capacity, or the number of elements it will hold. To accomplish this, use the keyword **new**.

```
int[ ] arr = new int[5];
```

The code above declares an array of 5 integers.
In an array, the elements are ordered and each has a specific and constant position, which is called an **index**.

To reference elements in an array, type the name of the array followed by the index position within a pair of square brackets.

Example:

 arr[2] = 42;

This assigns a value of 42 to the element with 2 as its index.

Note : elements in the array are identified with **zero-based** index numbers, meaning that the first element's index is 0 rather than one. So, the maximum index of the array int[5] is 4.

3.0.1.1 **Initializing Arrays-**

Java provides a shortcut for instantiating arrays of primitive types and strings.
If you already know what values to insert into the array, you can use an **array literal**.
Example of an array literal:

```
String[ ] myNames = { "A", "B", "C", "D"};
System.out.println(myNames[2]);

// Outputs "C"
```

Place the values in a **comma-separated** list, enclosed in curly braces.
The code above automatically initializes an array containing 4 elements, and stores the provided values.

Note : Sometimes you might see the square brackets placed after the array name, which also works, but the preferred way is to place the brackets after the array's data type.

3.0.2 **Summing Elements in Arrays-**

3.0.2.1 Array Length

You can access the length of an array (the number of elements it stores) via its **length** property.
Example:

```java
int[ ] intArr = new int[5];
System.out.println(intArr.length);

//Outputs 5
```

Note : Don't forget that in arrays, indexes start from 0. So, in the example above, the last index is 4.

3.0.2.2 Arrays

Now that we know how to set and get array elements, we can calculate the sum of all elements in an array by using loops.
The **for** loop is the most used loop when working with arrays, as we can use the **length** of the array to determine how many times to run the loop

```java
int [] myArr = {6, 42, 3, 7};
int sum=0;
for(int x=0; x<myArr.length; x++) {
   sum += myArr[x];
}
System.out.println(sum);

// 58
```

.

In the code above, we declared a variable **sum** to store the result and assigned it 0.
Then we used a **for** loop to iterate through the array, and added each element's value to the variable.

Note : The condition of the **for** loop is x<myArr.length, as the last element's index is **myArr.length-1**.

3.0.3 **Enhanced For Loop**

The **enhanced for loop** (sometimes called a "for each" loop) is used to traverse elements in arrays.

The advantages are that it eliminates the possibility of bugs and makes the code easier to read.

Example:

```
int[ ] primes = {2, 3, 5, 7};

for (int t: primes) {
   System.out.println(t);
}

/*
2
3
5
7
*/
```

The **enhanced for loop** declares a variable of a type compatible with the elements of the array being accessed. The variable will be available within the **for** block, and its value will be the same as the current array element.

So, on each iteration of the loop, the variable **t** will be equal to the corresponding element in the array.

Note : The **colon** after the variable in the syntax.

3.0.4 Multidimensional Arrays

Multidimensional arrays are array that contain other arrays. The two-dimensional array is the most basic multidimensional array.

To create multidimensional arrays, place each array within its own set of square brackets.

Example of a two-dimensional array:

int[ ][ ] sample = { {1, 2, 3}, {4, 5, 6} };

This declares an array with two arrays as its elements.
To access an element in the two-dimensional array, provide two indexes, one for the array, and another for the element inside that array.
The following example accesses the first element in the second array of sample.

```
int x = sample[1][0];
System.out.println(x);
```

// Outputs 4

Note : The array's two indexes are called **row index** and **column index**.

You can get and set a multidimensional array's elements using the same pair of square brackets.
Example:

```
int[ ][ ] myArr = { {1, 2, 3}, {4}, {5, 6, 7} };
myArr[0][2] = 42;
int x = myArr[1][0]; // 4
```

The above two-dimensional array contains three arrays. The first array has three elements, the second has a single element and the last of these has three elements.

Note : In Java, you're not limited to just two-dimensional arrays. Arrays can be nested within arrays to as many levels as your program needs. All you need to declare an array with more than two dimensions, is to add as many sets of empty brackets as you need. However, these are harder to maintain.
Remember, that all array members must be of the same type.

3.0.5 Quiz-003

Q.1. What is the output of this code?

```java
int arr[ ] = new int[3];
for (int i = 0; i < 3; i++) {
arr[i] = i;
}
int res = arr[0] + arr[2];
System.out.println(res);
```

Ans:

Q.2. What is the output of this code?

```java
int result = 0;
for (int i = 0; i < 5; i++) {
if (i == 3) {
result += 10;
} else {
result += i;
}
}
System.out.println(result);
```

Ans:

Q.3. Fill in the blanks to calculate the sum of all elements in the array "arr" using an enhanced for loop:

```
int res = 0;

[          ]

(int el

[          ]

 arr) {
  res +=

[          ]

;
}
```

Chapter 4 – Classes & Objects

4.0.1 Object Oriented Programming- OOP

Java uses **O**bject-**O**riented **P**rogramming (OOP), a programming style that is intended to make thinking about programming closer to thinking about the real world.
In OOP, each object is an independent unit with a **unique identity**, just as objects in the real world are.

An apple is an object; so is a mug. Each has its unique **identity**. It's possible to have two mugs that look identical, but they are still separate, unique objects.

Objects also have **characteristics**, which are used to describe them.
For example, a car can be red or blue, a mug can be full or empty, and so on. These characteristics are also called **attributes**. An attribute describes the current state of an object.
In the real world, each object behaves in its own way. The car moves, the phone rings, and so on.
The same applies to objects: **behavior** is specific to the object's type.

In summary, in object oriented programming, each object has three dimensions: **identity**, **attributes**, and **behavior**.
Attributes describe the object's current state, and what the object is capable of doing is demonstrated through the object's behavior.

4.0.1.1 Classes

A class describes what the object will be, but is separate from the object itself.

In other words, classes can be described as blueprints, descriptions, or definitions for an object. You can use the same class as a blueprint for creating multiple objects. The first step is to define the class, which then becomes a blueprint for object creation.

Each class has a name, and each is used to define attributes and behavior.

Some examples of attributes and behavior:

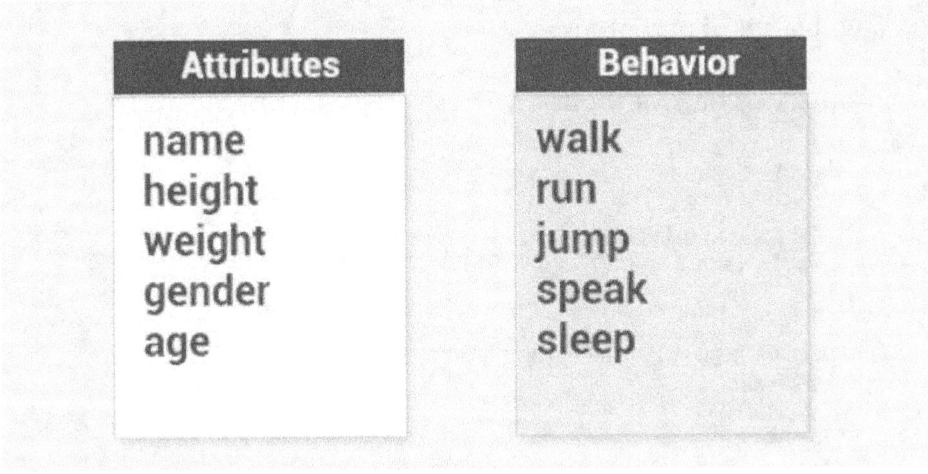

In other words, an object is an instance of a class.

4.0.2 **Methods-**

Methods define **behavior**. A method is a collection of statements that are grouped together to perform an operation.
System.out.println() is an example of a method.
You can define your own methods to perform your desired tasks.
Let's consider the following code:

```java
class MyClass {

  static void sayHello() {
    System.out.println("Hello World!");
  }

  public static void main(String[ ] args) {
    sayHello();
  }
}
// Outputs "Hello World!"
```

The code above declares a method called "sayHello", which prints a text, and then gets called in **main**.

Note : To call a method, type its name and then follow the name with a set of parentheses.

4.0.2.1 **Calling Methods-**

```java
class MyClass {

  static void sayHello() {
    System.out.println("Hello World!");
  }

  public static void main(String[ ] args) {
    sayHello();
    sayHello();
    sayHello();
  }
}

// Hello World!
// Hello World!
// Hello World!
```

Note : In cases like the one above, where the same thing is repeated over and over, you can achieve the same result using loops (while or for).

4.0.2.2 **Method Parameters-**

You can also create a method that takes some data, called **parameters**, along with it when you call it. Write parameters within the method's parentheses.

For example, we can modify our **sayHello**() method to take and output a **String** parameter.

```java
class MyClass {

  static void sayHello(String name) {
    System.out.println("Hello " + name);
  }

  public static void main(String[] args) {
    sayHello("David");
    sayHello("Amy");
  }

}
// Hello David
// Hello Amy
```

The method above takes a String called **name** as a parameter, which is used in the method's body. Then, when calling the method, we pass the parameter's value inside the parentheses. Methods can take multiple, comma-separated parameters.

The advantages of using methods instead of simple statements include the following:
- **code reuse**: You can write a method once, and use it multiple times, without having to rewrite the code each time.
- **parameters**: Based on the parameters passed in, methods can perform various actions.

4.0.3 **Method Return Type-**

4.0.3.1 The Return Type
The **return** keyword can be used in methods to return a value.
For example, we could define a method named **sum** that returns the sum of its two parameters.

```
static int sum(int val1, int val2) {
return val1 + val2;
}
```

Notice that in the method definition, we defined the **return type** before we defined the method name. For our sum method, it is **int**, as it takes two parameters of the type **int** and returns their sum, which is also an **int**.

The **static** keyword will be discussed in a future lesson.

Now, we can use the method in our main.

```
class MyClass {

static int sum(int val1, int val2) {
  return val1 + val2;
}

  public static void main(String[ ] args) {
    int x = sum(2, 5);
    System.out.println(x);
  }
}
// Outputs "7"
```

As the method returns a value, we can assign it to a variable.

Note : When you do not need to return any value from your method, use the keyword **void**.

Notice the **void** keyword in the definition of the main method - this means that main does not return anything.

Take a look at the same code from our previous lesson with explaining comments, so you can better understand how it works:

```java
// returns an int value 5
static int returnFive() {
  return 5;
}

// has a parameter
static void sayHelloTo(String name) {
  System.out.println("Hello " + name);
}

// simply prints"Hello World!"
static void sayHello() {
  System.out.println("Hello World!");
}
```

Having gained knowledge of method return types and parameters, let's take another look at the definition of the main method.

public static **void** main(String[ ] args)

Note : This definition indicates that the **main** method takes an array of Strings as its parameters, and does not return a value.

Let's create a method that takes two parameters of type **int** and returns the greater one, then call it in **main**:

```java
public static void main(String[ ] args) {
  int res = max(7, 42);
  System.out.println(res); //42
}

static int max(int a, int b) {
  if(a > b) {
    return a;
  }
  else {
    return b;
  }
}
```

Note : A method can have one type of parameter (or parameters) and return another, different type. For example, it can take two doubles and return an int.

4.0.4 Creating Classes and Objects

4.0.4.1 Creating Classes

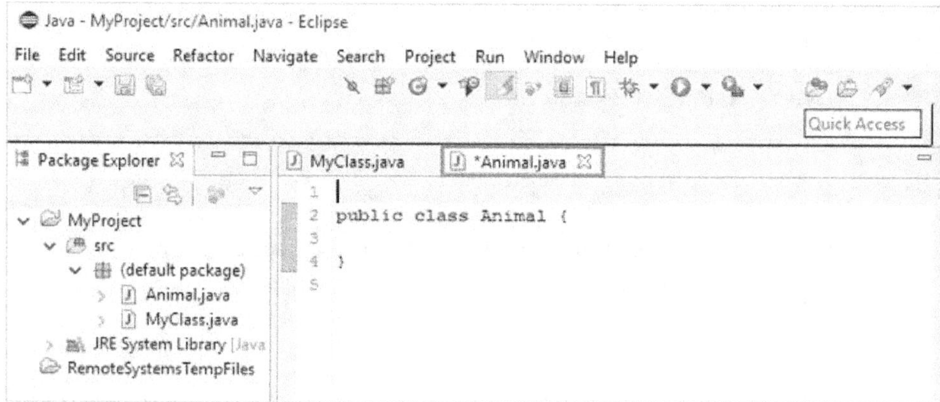

As you can see, Eclipse has already added the initial code for the class.

Now lets create a simple method in our new class.

Animal.java

```java
public class Animal {
void bark() {
System.out.println("Woof-Woof");
}
}
```

We declared a **bark()** method in our **Animal** class.

Note : Now, in order to use the class and it's methods, we need to declare an **object** of that class.

4.0.4.2 Creating Objects

Let's head over to our **main** and create a new object of our class.

MyClass.java

```java
class MyClass {
  public static void main(String[] args) {
    Animal dog = new Animal();
    dog.bark();
  }
}
// Outputs "Woof-Woof"
```

Now, **dog** is an object of type **Animal**. Thus we can call its **bark**() method, using the name of the object and a **dot**.

The **dot** notation is used to access the object's **attributes** and **methods**.

You have just created your first object!

4.0.5 Classes Attributes

4.0.5.1 Defining attributes

A class has **attributes** and **methods**. The attributes are basically variables within a class.

Let's create a class called **Vehicle**, with its corresponding attributes and methods.

```java
public class Vehicle {
  int maxSpeed;
  int wheels;
  String color;
  double fuelCapacity;

  void horn() {
    System.out.println("Beep!");
  }
}
```

maxSpeed, **wheels**, **color**, and **fuelCapacity** are the attributes of our Vehicle class, and **horn()** is the only method.

Note : You can define as many attributes and methods as necessary.

4.0.5.2 Creating Objects

Next, we can create multiple objects of our **Vehicle** class, and use the dot syntax to access their attributes and methods.

```
class MyClass {
  public static void main(String[ ] args) {
    Vehicle v1 = new Vehicle();
    Vehicle v2 = new Vehicle();
    v1.color = "red";
    v2.horn();
  }
}
```

Note : Try It Yourself to play around with the code!

4.0.6 Access Modifiers

Now let's discuss the **public** keyword in front of the main method.

public static void main(String[ ] args)

public is an **access modifier**, meaning that it is used to set the level of access. You can use access modifiers for classes, attributes, and methods.

For classes, the available modifiers are public or default (left blank), as described below:
public: The class is accessible by any other class.
default: The class is accessible only by classes in the same package.

The following choices are available for attributes and methods:
default: A variable or method declared with no access control

modifier is available to any other class in the same package.

public: Accessible from any other class.

protected: Provides the same access as the default access modifier, with the addition that subclasses can access protected methods and variables of the superclass (Subclasses and superclasses are covered in upcoming lessons).

private: Accessible only within the declared class itself.

Example:

```java
public class Vehicle {
  private int maxSpeed;
  private int wheels;
  private String color;
  private double fuelCapacity;

  public void horn() {
    System.out.println("Beep!");
  }
}
```

Note : It's a best practice to keep the variables within a class private. The variables are accessible and modified using **Getters** and **Setters**.

Tap **Continue** to learn about Getters and Setters.

4.0.7 Getters and Setters

Getters and **Setters** are used to effectively protect your data, particularly when creating classes. For each variable, the **get** method returns its value, while the **set** method sets the value.

Getters start with **get**, followed by the variable name, with the first letter of the variable name capitalized.

Setters start with **set**, followed by the variable name, with the first letter of the variable name capitalized.

Example:

```java
public class Vehicle {
  private String color;

  // Getter
  public String getColor() {
    return color;
  }

  // Setter
  public void setColor(String c) {
    this.color = c;
  }
}
```

The **getter** method returns the value of the attribute.
The **setter** method takes a parameter and assigns it to the attribute.

Note : The keyword **this** is used to refer to the current object. Basically, **this.color** is the **color** attribute of the current object.

Once our getter and setter have been defined, we can use it in our **main**:

```java
public static void main(String[ ] args) {
  Vehicle v1 = new Vehicle();
  v1.setColor("Red");
  System.out.println(v1.getColor());
}

//Outputs "Red"
```

Getters and setters allow us to have control over the values. You may, for example, validate the given value in the setter before actually setting the value.

Note : Getters and setters are fundamental building blocks for **encapsulation**, which will be covered in the next module.

4.0.8 Constructors

Constructors are special methods invoked when an object is created and are used to initialize them.

A constructor can be used to provide initial values for object attributes.

- A constructor name must be same as its class name.
- A constructor must have no explicit return type.

Example of a constructor:

```java
public class Vehicle {
  private String color;
  Vehicle() {
    color = "Red";
  }
}
```

The **Vehicle**() method is the constructor of our class, so whenever an object of that class is created, the color attribute will be set to "Red".

A constructor can also take parameters to initialize attributes.

```java
public class Vehicle {
  private String color;
  Vehicle(String c) {
    color = c;
  }
}
```

Note : You can think of constructors as methods that will set up your class by default, so you don't need to repeat the same code every time.

4.0.8.1 Using Constructors

The constructor is called when you create an object using the **new** keyword.

Example:

```java
public class MyClass {
  public static void main(String[ ] args) {
    Vehicle v = new Vehicle("Blue");
  }
}
```

Note : This will call the constructor, which will set the **color** attribute to "Blue".

Example:

```java
public class Vehicle {
  private String color;

  Vehicle() {
    this.setColor("Red");
  }
  Vehicle(String c) {
    this.setColor(c);
  }

  // Setter
  public void setColor(String c) {
    this.color = c;
  }
}
```

The class above has two constructors, one without any parameters setting the color attribute to a default value of "Red", and another constructor that accepts a parameter and assigns it to the attribute.

Now, we can use the constructors to create objects of our class.

```java
//color will be "Red"
Vehicle v1 = new Vehicle();
```

```java
//color will be "Green"
Vehicle v2 = new Vehicle("Green");
```

Note : Java automatically provides a default constructor, so all classes have a constructor, whether one is specifically defined or not.

4.0.9 **Value and Reference Types**

4.0.9.1 Value Types

Value types are the basic types, and include byte, short, int, long, float, double, boolean, and char.
These data types store the values assigned to them in the corresponding memory locations.
So, when you pass them to a method, you basically operate on the variable's **value**, rather than on the variable itself.
Example:

```java
public class MyClass {
  public static void main(String[ ] args) {
    int x = 5;
    addOneTo(x);
    System.out.println(x);
  }
  static void addOneTo(int num) {
    num = num + 1;
  }
}
// Outputs "5"
```

Note : The method from the example above takes the **value** of its parameter, which is why the original variable is not affected and 5 remains as its value.

4.0.9.2 Reference Type

A **reference type** stores a reference (or address) to the memory location where the corresponding data is stored.
When you create an object using the constructor, you create a reference variable.
For example, consider having a Person class defined:

```java
public class MyClass {
  public static void main(String[ ] args) {
    Person j;
    j = new Person("John");
    j.setAge(20);
    celebrateBirthday(j);
    System.out.println(j.getAge());
  }
  static void celebrateBirthday(Person p) {
    p.setAge(p.getAge() + 1);
  }
}
//Outputs "21"
```

The method **celebrateBirthday** takes a Person object as its parameter, and increments its attribute.

Because **j** is a reference type, the method affects the object itself, and is able to change the actual value of its attribute.

Note : Arrays and **Strings** are also reference data types.

4.0.10 **The Math Class-**

The **JDK** defines a number of useful classes, one of them being the **Math** class, which provides predefined methods for mathematical operations.

You do not need to create an object of the **Math** class to use it. To access it, just type in **Math.** and the corresponding method.

Math.abs() returns the absolute value of its parameter.

```java
int a = Math.abs(10); // 10
int b = Math.abs(-20); // 20
```

Math.ceil() rounds a floating point value up to the nearest integer value. The rounded value is returned as a **double**.

double c = Math.ceil(7.342); // 8.0

Similarly, **Math.floor()** rounds a floating point value down to the nearest integer value.

double f = Math.floor(7.343); // 7.0

Math.max() returns the largest of its parameters.

int m = Math.max(10, 20); // 20

Conversely, **Math.min()** returns the smallest parameter.

int m = Math.min(10, 20); // 10

Math.pow() takes two parameters and returns the first parameter raised to the power of the second parameter.

double p = Math.pow(2, 3); // 8.0

Note : There are a number of other methods available in the Math class, including:
sqrt() for square root, **sin() for** sine, **cos() for** cosine, and others.

4.0.11 **Static-**

When you declare a variable or a method as **static**, it belongs to the class, rather than to a specific instance. This means that only one instance of a **static** member exists, even if you create multiple objects of the class, or if you don't create any. It will be shared by all objects.
Example:

```java
public class Counter {
  public static int COUNT=0;
  Counter() {
    COUNT++;
  }
}
```

The **COUNT** variable will be shared by all objects of that class. Now, we can create objects of our Counter class in **main**, and access the static variable.

```java
public class MyClass {
  public static void main(String[ ] args) {
    Counter c1 = new Counter();
    Counter c2 = new Counter();
    System.out.println(Counter.COUNT);
  }
}
//Outputs "2"
```

The output is 2, because the **COUNT** variable is static and gets incremented by one each time a new object of the Counter class is created. In the code above, we created 2 objects.
You can also access the static variable using any object of that class, such as **c1.COUNT**.

Note : It's a common practice to use upper case when naming a static variable, although not mandatory.

The same concept applies to **static** methods.

```java
public class Vehicle {
public static void horn() {
System.out.println("Beep");
}
}
```

Now, the **horn** method can be called without creating an object:

```
public class MyClass {
public static void main(String[ ] args) {
Vehicle.horn();
}
}
```

Another example of static methods are those of the **Math** class, which is why you can call them without creating a **Math** object.

Note : Also, the **main** method must always be **static**.

4.0.12 **Final-**

Use the **final** keyword to mark a variable constant, so that it can be assigned only once.

Example:

```
class MyClass {
  public static final double PI = 3.14;
  public static void main(String[ ] args) {
    System.out.println(PI);
  }
}
```

PI is now a constant. Any attempt to assign it a value will cause an error.

Note : Methods and classes can also be marked **final**. This serves to restrict methods so that they can't be overridden and classes so that they can't be subclassed.
These concepts will be covered in the next module.

4.0.13 **Packages-**

Packages are used to avoid name conflicts and to control access to classes.
A **package** can be defined as a group made up of similar types of

classes, along with sub-packages.

Creating a package in Java is quite easy. Simply right click on your **src** directory and click New->Package. Give your package a name and click **Finish**.

You will notice that the new package appears in the project directory. Now you can move and create classes inside that package. We have moved our **Vehicle**, **Counter** and **Animal** classes to the package **samples**.

When you move/create a class in your

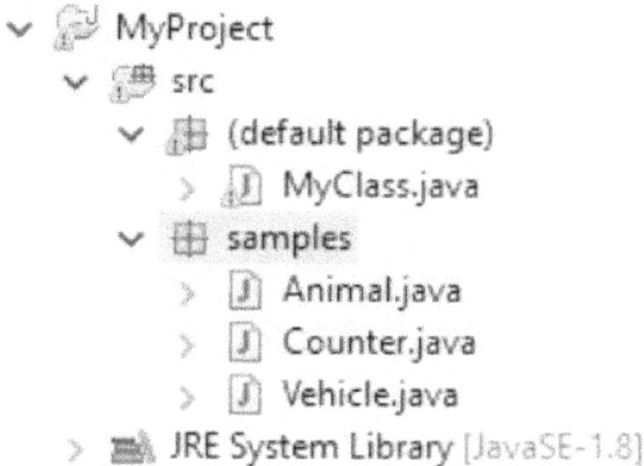

 package, the following code will appear at the top of the list of files.

package samples;

This indicates the package to which the class belongs.

Now, we need to import the classes that are inside a package in our main to be able to use them.

The following example shows how to use the **Vehicle** class of the **samples** package.

```
import samples.Vehicle;

class MyClass {
  public static void main(String[ ] args) {
    Vehicle v1 = new Vehicle();
    v1.horn();
  }
}
```

Two major results occur when a class is placed in a package. First, the name of the package becomes a part of the name of the class. Second, the name of the package must match the directory structure where the corresponding class file resides.

Note : Use a wildcard to import all classes in a package.
For example, **import samples.*** will import all classes in the samples package.

4.0.14 **Quiz-004-**

Q.1. Fill in the blank to define a method that does not return a value.

Public____calc()

Q.2. Which access modifier explicitly says that a method or variable of an object can be accessed by code from outside of the class of that object?

- static
- default
- private
- public

Q.3. Arrange the code to declare a method returning the greater of the two arguments.

return b;	if (a > b){	return a; }	public int max(int

a, int b) {   }

Q.4. Fill in the blanks to declare a method that takes one argument of type int.

```
public int myFunc(____ x)
   return x*10;
```

____

Q.5. Fill in the blanks to create a method that returns the minimum of the two parameters.

```
public int minFunc(int n1, int n2 ______
{
   int min;
   if (n1 > n2)
      min = ______

   ______

;
      min = n1;

______ min;
}
```

Q.6. Fill in the blanks to create a class with a method called "myFunc" that takes no parameters, returns void, and prints "Hi" to the screen.

```
public _____ myClass

  public_____ myFunc

{

  System.out.println("Hi");

  }

}
```

Chapter 5 – Classes- A brief Description

5.0.1 Encapsulation-

There are 4 core concepts in Object Oriented Programming -OOP:
encapsulation, **inheritance**, **polymorphism**, and **abstraction**.
The idea behind **encapsulation** is to ensure that implementation
details are not visible to users. The variables of one class will be
hidden from the other classes, accessible only through the
methods of the current class. This is called **data hiding**.
To achieve encapsulation in Java, declare the class' variables as
private and provide public **setter** and **getter** methods to modify
and view the variables' values.

For example:

```java
class BankAccount {
  private double balance=0;
  public void deposit(double x) {
    if(x > 0) {
      balance += x;
    }
  }
}
```

This implementation hides the **balance** variable, enabling access to it only through the **deposit** method, which validates the amount to be deposited before modifying the variable.

Note : In summary, **encapsulation** provides the following benefits:
- Control of the way data is accessed or modified
- More flexible and easily changed code
- Ability to change one part of the code without affecting other parts

5.0.2 **Inheritance**-

Inheritance is the process that enables one class to acquire the properties (methods and variables) of another. With inheritance, the information is placed in a more manageable, hierarchical order.
The class inheriting the properties of another is the **subclass** (also called derived class, or child class); the class whose properties are inherited is the **superclass** (base class, or parent class).
To inherit from a class, use the **extends** keyword.
This example shows how to have the class **Dog** to inherit from the class **Animal**.

```
class Dog extends Animal {
// some code
}
```

Note : Here, Dog is the **subclass**, and Animal is the **superclass**.

When one class is inherited from another class, it inherits all of the superclass' **non-private** variables and methods.
Example:

```java
class Animal {
  protected int legs;
  public void eat() {
    System.out.println("Animal eats");
  }
}

class Dog extends Animal {
  Dog() {
    legs = 4;
  }
}
```

As you can see, the Dog class inherits the legs variable from the Animal class.

We can now declare a Dog object and call the **eat** method of its superclass:

Note :Recall the **protected** access modifier, which makes the members visible only to the subclasses.

Constructors are not member methods, and so are not inherited by subclasses.

However, the constructor of the superclass is called when the subclass is instantiated.

Example:

```java
class A {
  public A() {
    System.out.println("New A");
  }
}
class B extends A {
  public B() {
    System.out.println("New B");
  }
}

class Program {
  public static void main(String[] args) {
    B obj = new B();
  }
}

/*Outputs
"New A"
"New B"
*/
```

Note : You can access the superclass from the subclass using the **super** keyword.

For example, **super.var** accesses the var member of the superclass.

5.0.3 **Polymorphism-**

Polymorphism, which refers to the idea of "having many forms", occurs when there is a hierarchy of classes related to each other through inheritance.

A call to a member method will cause a different implementation to be executed, depending on the type of the object invoking the method.

Here is an example: **Dog** and **Cat** are classes that inherit from the **Animal** class. Each class has its own implementation of the **makeSound**() method.

```java
class Animal {
  public void makeSound() {
    System.out.println("Grr...");
  }
}
class Cat extends Animal {
  public void makeSound() {
    System.out.println("Meow");
  }
}
class Dog extends Animal {
  public void makeSound() {
    System.out.println("Woof");
  }
}
```

As all **Cat** and **Dog** objects are **Animal** objects, we can do the following in **main**:

```java
public static void main(String[ ] args) {
  Animal a = new Dog();
  Animal b = new Cat();
}
```

We've created two reference variables of type Animal, and pointed them to the **Cat** and **Dog** objects.
Now, we can call the makeSound() methods.

```java
a.makeSound();
//Outputs "Woof"

b.makeSound();
//Outputs "Meow"
```

As the reference variable **a** contains a Dog object, the makeSound() method of the Dog class will be called.
The same applies to the **b** variable.

Note : This demonstrates that you can use the **Animal** variable without actually knowing that it contains an object of the subclass.

This is very useful when you have multiple subclasses of the superclass.

5.0.4 **Overriding & Overloading-**

5.0.4.1 Method Overriding

As we saw in the previous lesson, a subclass can define a behavior that's specific to the subclass type, meaning that a subclass can implement a parent class method based on its requirement.

This feature is known as method **overriding**.

Example:

```java
class Animal {
   public void makeSound() {
      System.out.println("Grr...");
   }
}
class Cat extends Animal {
   public void makeSound() {
      System.out.println("Meow");
   }
}
```

In the code above, the Cat class overrides the **makeSound**() method of its superclass Animal.

Rules for Method Overriding:

- Should have the **same** return type and arguments
- The **access level** cannot be more restrictive than the overridden method's access level (Example: If the superclass method is declared public, the overriding method in the sub class can be neither private nor protected)
- A method declared **final** or **static** cannot be overridden
- If a method cannot be inherited, it cannot be overridden

- Constructors cannot be overridden.

Note : Method overriding is also known as **runtime polymorphism**.

5.0.4.2 Method Overloading-

When methods have the same name, but different parameters, it is known as method **overloading**.
This can be very useful when you need the same method functionality for different types of parameters.
The following example illustrates a method that returns the maximum of its two parameters

```
int max(int a, int b) {
  if(a > b) {
    return a;
  }
  else {
    return b;
  }
}
```

The method shown above will only work for parameters of type **integer**.
However, we might want to use it for **doubles**, as well. For that, you need to overload the **max** method:

```
double max(double a, double b) {
  if(a > b) {
    return a;
  }
  else {
    return b;
  }
}
```

Now, our **max** method will also work with **doubles**.
An overloaded method **must** have a different argument list; the

parameters should differ in their type, number, or both.

Note : Another name for method overloading is **compile-time polymorphism**.

5.0.5 **Abstract Classes-**

Data **abstraction** provides the outside world with only essential information, in a process of representing essential features without including implementation details.
A good real-world example is a *book*. When you hear the term book, you don't know the exact specifics, such as the page count, the color, or the size, but you understand the idea, or abstraction, of a book.
The concept of **abstraction** is that we focus on essential qualities, rather than the specific characteristics of one particular example.

In Java, abstraction is achieved using **abstract classes** and **interfaces**.
An abstract class is defined using the **abstract** keyword.
- If a class is declared abstract it cannot be instantiated (you cannot create objects of that type).
- To use an abstract class, you have to inherit it from another class.
- Any class that contains an abstract method should be defined as abstract.

Note : An abstract method is a method that is declared without an implementation (without braces, and followed by a semicolon):
abstract void walk();

For example, we can define our Animal class as abstract:

```
abstract class Animal {
  int legs = 0;
  abstract void makeSound();
}
```

The makeSound method is also abstract, as it has no implementation in the superclass.

We can inherit from the Animal class and define the makeSound() method for the subclass:

```
class Cat extends Animal {
  public void makeSound() {
    System.out.println("Meow");
  }
}
```

Note : Every Animal makes a sound, but each has a different way to do it. That's why we define an abstract class Animal, and leave the implementation of how they make sounds to the subclasses. This is used when there is no meaningful definition for the method in the superclass.

5.0.6 Interfaces-

An **interface** is a completely abstract class that contains only abstract methods.

Some specifications for interfaces:

- Defined using the **interface** keyword.

- May contain only static final variables.

- Cannot contain a constructor because interfaces cannot be instantiated.

- Interfaces can extend other interfaces.

- A class can implement any number of interfaces.

An example of a simple interface:

```java
interface Animal {
  public void eat();
  public void makeSound();
}
```

Interfaces have the following properties:

- An interface is implicitly abstract. You do not need to use the abstract keyword while declaring an interface.

- Each method in an interface is also implicitly abstract, so the abstract keyword is not needed.

- Methods in an interface are implicitly public.

Note : A class can inherit from just **one** superclass, but can implement **multiple** interfaces!

Use the **implements** keyword to use an interface with your class.

```java
interface Animal {
  public void eat();
  public void makeSound();
}

class Cat implements Animal {
  public void makeSound() {
    System.out.println("Meow");
  }
  public void eat() {
    System.out.println("omnomnom");
  }
}
```

Note : When you implement an interface, you need to override all of its methods.

5.0.7 **Casting**-

Assigning a value of one type to a variable of another type is known as **Type Casting**.
To cast a value to a specific type, place the type in parentheses and position it in front of the value.

Example:

```
int a = (int) 3.14;
System.out.println(a);
//Outputs 3
```

The code above is casting the value 3.14 to an integer, with 3 as the resulting value.

Another example:

```
double a = 42.571;
int b = (int) a;
System.out.println(b);
//Outputs 42
```

Note : Java supports automatic type casting of integers to floating points, since there is no loss of precision.
On the other hand, type casting is mandatory when assigning floating point values to integer variables.

5.0.8 Downcasting-

For classes, there are two types of casting.

<u>Upcasting</u>

You can cast an instance of a subclass to its superclass.

Consider the following example, assuming that Cat is a subclass of Animal.

```
Animal a = new Cat();
```

Java automatically upcasted the Cat type variable to the Animal type.

Downcasting

Casting an object of a superclass to its subclass is called downcasting.

Example:

```
Animal a = new Cat();
((Cat)a).makeSound();
```

This will try to cast the variable a to the **Cat** type and call its makeSound() method.

Note : Why is upcasting automatic, downcasting manual? Well, upcasting can never fail. But if you have a group of different Animals and want to downcast them all to a Cat, then there's a chance that some of these Animals are actually Dogs, so the process fails.

5.0.9 Anonymous Classes-

Anonymous classes are a way to extend the existing classes on the fly.
For example, consider having a class Machine:

```
class Machine {
  public void start() {
    System.out.println("Starting...");
  }
}
```

When creating the Machine object, we can change the start method on the fly.

```
public static void main(String[] args) {
  Machine m = new Machine() {
    @Override public void start() {
      System.out.println("Wooooo");
    }
  };
  m.start();
}
//Outputs "Wooooo";
```

After the constructor call, we have opened the curly braces and have overridden the **start** method's implementation on the fly.

Note : The **@Override** annotation is used to make your code easier to understand, because it makes it more obvious when methods are overridden.

The modification is applicable only to the current object, and not the class itself. So if we create another object of that class, the start method's implementation will be the one defined in the class.

```
class Machine {
  public void start() {
    System.out.println("Starting...");
  }
}
public static void main(String[] args) {
  Machine m1 = new Machine() {
    @Override public void start() {
      System.out.println("Wooooo");
    }
  };
  Machine m2 = new Machine();
  m2.start();
}
//Outputs "Starting..."
```

Note : Tap **Try It Yourself** to play around with the code!

5.0.10 Inner Classes

Java supports **nesting** classes; a class can be a member of another class.

Creating an inner class is quite simple. Just write a class within a class. Unlike a class, an inner class can be private. Once you declare an inner class private, it cannot be accessed from an object outside the class.

Example:

```java
class Robot {
  int id;
  Robot(int i) {
    id = i;
    Brain b = new Brain();
    b.think();
  }

  private class Brain {
    public void think() {
      System.out.println(id + " is thinking");
    }
  }

}
```

Note : The class **Robot** has an inner class **Brain**. The inner class can access all of the member variables and methods of its outer class, but it cannot be accessed from any outside class.

5.0.11 The equal() Method

5.0.11.1 **Comparing Object-**

Remember that when you create objects, the variables store references to the objects.

So, when you compare objects using the equality testing operator (==), it actually compares the references and not the object values.

Example:

```java
class Animal {
  String name;
  Animal(String n) {
    name = n;
  }
}

class MyClass {
  public static void main(String[ ] args) {
    Animal a1 = new Animal("Robby");
    Animal a2 = new Animal("Robby");
    System.out.println(a1 == a2);
  }
}
//Outputs false
```

Note : Despite having two objects with the same name, the equality testing returns false, because we have two different objects (two different references or memory locations).

5.0.11.2 equals()-

Each object has a predefined **equals**() method that is used for semantical equality testing.

But, to make it work for our classes, we need to override it and check the conditions we need.

There is a simple and fast way of generating the equals() method, other than writing it manually.

Just right click in your class, go to **Source->Generate hashCode() and equals().**

Open With	>		Override/Implement Methods...
Show In	Alt+Shift+W >		Generate Getters and Setters...
Cut	Ctrl+X		Generate Delegate Methods...
Copy	Ctrl+C		Generate hashCode() and equals()...
Copy Qualified Name			Generate toString()...
Paste	Ctrl+V		Generate Constructor using Fields...
Quick Fix	Ctrl+1		Generate Constructors from Superclass...
Source	Alt+Shift+S >		Externalize Strings...
Refactor	Alt+Shift+T >		

This will automatically create the necessary methods.

```java
class Animal {
  String name;
  Animal(String n) {
    name = n;
  }
  @Override
  public int hashCode() {
    final int prime = 31;
    int result = 1;
    result = prime * result + ((name == null) ? 0 : name.hashCode());
    return result;
  }
  @Override
  public boolean equals(Object obj) {
    if (this == obj)
      return true;
    if (obj == null)
      return false;
    if (getClass() != obj.getClass())
      return false;
    Animal other = (Animal) obj;
    if (name == null) {
      if (other.name != null)
        return false;
    } else if (!name.equals(other.name))
      return false;
    return true;
  }
}
```

The automatically generated hashCode() method is used to determine where to store the object internally. Whenever you implement **equals**, you MUST also implement **hashCode**.
We can run the test again, using the **equals** method:

```java
public static void main(String[ ] args) {
  Animal a1 = new Animal("Robby");
  Animal a2 = new Animal("Robby");
  System.out.println(a1.equals(a2));
}
//Outputs true
```

Note : You can use the same menu to generate other useful methods, such as **getters** and **setters** for your class attributes.

5.0.12 **Enums-**

An Enum is a special type used to define collections of constants.
Here is a simple Enum example:

```
enum Rank {
SOLDIER,
SERGEANT,
CAPTAIN
}
```

Note that the values are **comma-separated.**
You can refer to the constants in the enum above with the **dot** syntax.

```
Rank a = Rank.SOLDIER;
```

Note : Basically, Enums define variables that represent members of a fixed set.

After declaring an Enum, we can check for the corresponding values with, for example, a **switch** statement.

```
Rank a = Rank.SOLDIER;

switch(a) {
  case SOLDIER:
   System.out.println("Soldier says hi!");
   break;
  case SERGEANT:
   System.out.println("Sergeant says Hello!");
  break;
  case CAPTAIN:
   System.out.println("Captain says Welcome!");
   break;
}
//Outputs "Soldier says hi!"
```

Note : Tap **Try It Yourself** to play around with the code!

You should always use Enums when a variable (especially a

method parameter) can only take one out of a small set of possible values.

If you use Enums instead of integers (or String codes), you increase compile-time checking and avoid errors from passing in invalid constants, and you document which values are legal to use.

Note : Some sample Enum uses include month names, days of the week, deck of cards, etc..

5.0.13 Java API

The Java API is a collection of classes and interfaces that have been written for you to use.

The Java API Documentation with all of the available APIs can be located on the Oracle website at

http://docs.oracle.com/javase/7/docs/api/

Once you locate the package you want to use, you need to import it into your code.

The package can be imported using the import keyword.

For example:

import java.awt.*;

The **awt** package contains all of the classes for creating user interfaces and for painting graphics and images.

Note : The wildcard character (*) is used to import all of the classes in the package.

5.0.14 **Quiz-005**

```java
Q.1. What is the output of this code?
class A {
private void print() {
System.out.println("a");
}
private void print(String str) {
System.out.println("b");
}
private void print(int x) {
System.out.println("c");
}
public static void main(String[ ] args) {
A object = new A();
object.print(12);
}
}
```

Ans: _______________________________

Q.2. Fill in the blanks to define a new class Falcon, based on the superclass Bird.

_______Falcon _______ Bird {

}

Q.3. Object variables store.

Ans:

- Objects
- References
- Classes
- Strings

Q.4. What term is used for hiding the details of an object from the other parts of a program?

- Polymorphism
- Inheritance
- Encapsulation
- Data Mining

Q.5. A class Car and its subclass BMW each have a method run(), which was written by the developer as part of the class definition. If CarObj refers to an object of type BMW, what will CarObj.run(); do?

Ans:
- The compiler will complain that run() has been defined twice.
- The run() method defined in Car will be called.
- The run() method defined in BMW will be called.

Q.6. Valentine, Holiday, and Birthday inherit from the class Card. In order for the following code to be correct, what type must the reference variable card be?

card = new Valentine("A", 14) ;

card.greeting();

card = new Holiday("B") ;

card.greeting();

card = new Birthday("C", 12) ;

card.greeting();

Ans:

- Card
- Birthday
- Holiday
- Valentine